Whispers of the Soul

Beth McGowan

BookLeaf Publishing

India | USA | UK

Presentation by *BookLeaf Publishing*

Web: www.bookleafpub.com

E-mail: info@bookleafpub.com

ISBN: 9789358319958

First edition 2024

A letter to Mother

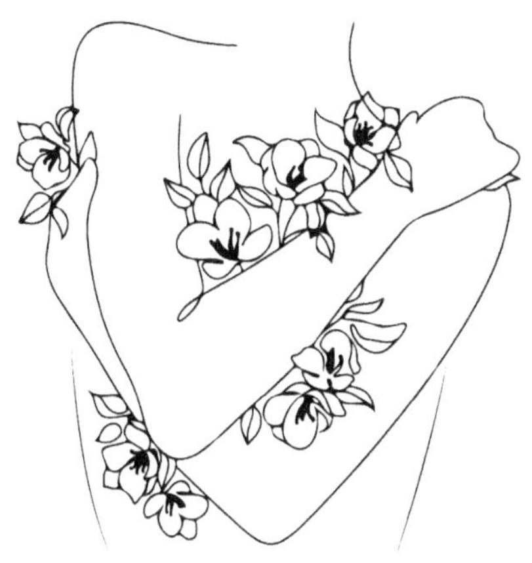

Dear Mother Nature,
I write to you today
In awe of your beauty,
In reverence I pray.

Your rivers and mountains.
Your forests so grand.
Your creatures so wondrous,
In every reach of this land.

But Mother, I worry,
For I see the pain you bear,
The scars on your surface,
The burden that you wear.

From the smog-filled cities,
To the melting ice caps.
Our actions, dear Mother,
Have caused such collapse.

We take and we take,
Without giving a thought,
To the fragile balance,
That your creation has sought.

The oceans are weeping,
Their tears filled with despair,
As plastic and pollution,
Choke the life that once was there.

The trees are shrinking,
Their leaves turning brown,
As deforestation spreads,
With zero signs of slowdown..

The animals are vanishing.
Their homes destroyed by sheer greed.
Their cries echo through the night,
A plea for us to take heed.

But Mother, there is hope,
In the hearts of those who care,
Who speak up for your rights,

And the future we must share.

We must change our ways,
And learn to coexist,
To protect and to nurture,
The gifts that you have kissed.

Let us heal your wounds,
With love and respect,
For it's in our hands,
To correct this neglect.

So, dear Mother Nature,
I offer this plea,
To cherish and to honour,
This world entrusted to me.

For without your beauty,
We are nothing at all,
So let us be grateful,
And answer your call.

With love and gratitude,
Your humble child, I stand,
Ready to protect you,
With every breath I command.

For you are the mother,
Who nurtures us all,
And it's time we remember,

To catch you when you fall.

Dear Mother Nature,
This letter I send,
In hopes that you'll forgive us,
And help us to mend.

For in your embrace,
We find solace and grace,
So let us be worthy,
Of this sacred space.

That's the thing about Technicolour

That's the thing about technicolour,
It paints our world with every vibrant hue.
Every shade, every tone, every shimmer,
A kaleidoscope of dreams come true.

In this realm of pixels and screens,
Where reality and fantasy collide,
Imagination knows no boundaries,
As our spirits take a joyful stride.

Gone are the days of black and white,
Now we bask in a vivid display.
From the deepest red to the brightest blue,
Our senses dance in a brilliant array.

But amidst this technicolour bliss,
We must not forget what lies beneath.
For colours alone cannot define,
The essence of life's tapestry, so brief.

So let us cherish this vibrant gift,
But also seek the beauty unseen.
For true wonder lies not only in colours,
But in the spaces in between.

That's the thing about technicolour,
It captures our hearts, our very core.
But let us remember, in this dazzling world,
The shades of grey that we adore.

Foggy beauty

A layer of fog, like a shroud, descends,
Softly embracing the world in its misty arms.
Veiling the landscape in a cloak of mystery.
Obscuring the familiar, inviting curiosity.

Through the haze, shapes emerge and dissolve,
A dance of shadows in this ethereal realm.
Silent whispers linger in the dampened air
As reality blurs, dreams awaken with flair.

The sun's warm touch, now a distant memory.
Muted colours, dulled by the fog's gentle touch.
Yet beauty lies within this atmospheric embrace
A canvas transformed in this transient space.

In this misty haven, time slows its pace.
The world hushed, as if caught in a trance.
A stillness that soothes the weary soul,
In this fleeting moment, peace takes its toll.

A layer of fog, a transient existence,
A reminder that life's mysteries persist.
Embracing the unknown, we wander through,
Lost in the beauty of this foggy view.

Grief

Grief, a silent visitor.
Unbidden, it arrives,
Unwanted, it lingers,
In the depths of our souls.

No rhyme or reason,
Just raw emotion.
A tumultuous sea,
Of sorrow and pain.

It clings to our hearts,
Like a shadow in the night.
Weighted with memories,
Of what once was.

In its presence,
Time stands still.
Days become endless.
Nights become void.

It steals our laughter,
Leaving behind tears.
Silencing our voices,
With a heavy sigh.

But within this grief,
Lies a glimmer of light,
A flicker of hope,
That someday, we'll heal.

For grief, though burdensome,
Is a testament to love,
To the beauty of connection,
And the bonds we hold dear.

So let us embrace it,
This unwelcome guest,
For it teaches us resilience,
And the strength to endure.

And as we navigate,
The depths of despair,
May we find solace,
In the healing power of time.

Grief, a haunting melody,
That echoes in our souls,
But in the symphony of life,
It is but one verse.

A cup of comfort

Steaming cup of tea,
Whispers of warmth on my lips,
Serenity sips.

A year gone by

One year has now passed,
Moments etched in memory,
Time's gentle embrace.

Spring's delicate bloom,
Whispers of hope and rebirth,
Awakening hearts.

Summer's golden rays,
Caress the earth and our souls,
Bathing us in light.

Autumn's fiery hues,
Nature's artistry on display,
Fading into slumber.

Winter's icy breath,
Silent whispers in the night,
Blanketing the world.

One year on, we stand,
Weathered, yet stronger within,
Resilient and true.

Through joy and sorrow,
Weaving a tapestry of life,
One year's precious gift.

Lessons learned, hearts healed,
The journey continues on,
With hope as our guide.

For in each passing year,
We find strength, love, and purpose,
The essence of life.

The little things

In the bustling whirl of life's grand schemes,
We often overlook the simplest things.
The tiny moments that hold the most grace,
In the rush, they're easy to erase.

But it's all in the little things, my friend,
The nuances that softly descend,
Like a gentle caress upon our soul,
They really can make us feel whole.

A tender smile from a passing stranger,
The warmth of coffee in the morning's danger,
The sound of laughter filling up the air,
These little things, they're everywhere.

The touch of a loved one's hand in ours,
The scent of rain on blooming flowers,
The taste of chocolate melting on our tongue,
These little things, they cannot be undone.

For in the grand tapestry of life's design,
It's the little things that truly shine,
They bring a sense of peace and delight,
And make the world seem oh so bright.

So let us cherish what may seem small,
For it's in these moments we stand tall,
For in the little things, we find our way,
To a life filled with joy, come what may.

Persistence

In life's great journey, there's a secret key,
A virtue rare, that sets the spirit free.
It's found within the hearts of those who dare,
To face each challenge with unwavering flair.

Persistence, like a flame that never dies,
Ignites the soul with dreams that touch the skies.
Through the darkest nights and stormy tempest's
wrath,
It guides us, lights the way along life's path.

When trials come, and doubts begin to rise,
Persistent souls will never compromise.
They forge ahead, undeterred by fear's grip,
With steadfast will, they never let it slip.

For dreams are born from those who persevere,
With passion burning bright, they have no fear.
Through every stumble, setback, or delay,
Their persistence ensures they'll find their way.

So let us learn from those who came before,
The ones who faced adversity and more,
In every challenge, let us find our stride,
And let our persistence be our guide.

For with each step, we'll inch toward,
Dreams just waiting to be explored.
Through ups and downs, we'll reach that distant
shore,
With persistence, we will soar.

Extinct.

In the depths of time, a creature did roam,
A bird of wonder, a legend of its own.
The dodo, they called it, with feathers so grand,
But fate had a plan, no mercy in hand.

Its wings were plump, unable to soar high,
A flightless wonder, under the vast blue sky.
With beady eyes and a clumsy gait,
The dodo danced, its end sealed by fate.

On an island paradise, its beautiful abode,
With no predators, the bird soon slowed.
Unaware of the danger that drew near,
The dodo thrived, void of any fear.

But man arrived, with a hunger to explore,
Unleashing havoc on this distant shore.
They hunted the dodo, for meat and for sport,
A tragic tale, where life was cut short.

The dodo's plumes, once vibrant and bright,
Faded away, lost in the endless night.
Its song silenced, forever untold,
As its existence turned to tales of old.

Now we remember, this bird of the past,
A symbol of extinction, a lesson to last.
The dodo's fate, a haunting reminder,
To cherish life's gifts, to be kinder.

Let us learn from this vanished bird,
To protect the creatures, a plea often heard.
For in their presence, we find our connection,
To the beauty of nature, a divine reflection.

So let us remember, the dodo's short tale,
And strive to ensure, no more species fail.
For in the loss of one, we all lose a part,
Of the intricate tapestry, that weaves our own
heart.

Mind over matter

In the realm of thoughts, where dreams take flight,
Resides a power, hidden from sight.
Mind over matter, a force untamed,
A catalyst for change, yet often unnamed.

With every thought, a universe is born,
A spark of creation, a path to be worn.
For in the mind, possibilities reside,
Where limitations falter, and dreams collide.

No walls too high, no barriers too vast,
When the mind soars, limitations are surpassed.
It whispers of courage, where fear once dwelled,
Empowering the spirit, where doubts were
expelled.

Mind over matter, a mantra to embrace,
A catalyst for growth, a life to retrace.
No longer confined by the chains of the past,
But rewriting the future, with dreams that will
last.

It beckons us forward, to break through the
mould,
To embrace the power we already hold.
To conquer the challenges that life may present,
With a mind keen, focused, and resolute, unbent.

So dare to dream, to believe in your might,
For mind over matter will change your life's
plight.
Unlock the potential, that within you lies,
With thoughts that can shape your own
boundless skies.

Procrastination

Procrastination, my dear old friend,
Whose grip on me I cannot mend.
In the realm of idle days I roam,
Lost in the abyss of my comfort zone.

Tomorrow's tasks can wait, I say,
As I while away the hours, day by day.
The urgency of time slips through my hands,
As I succumb to laziness' demands.

I promise myself, with each rising sun,
That today I'll conquer what needs to be done.
But distractions beckon, oh so sweet,
And my determination takes a backseat.

I find solace in the art of delay,
As minutes turn to hours and slip away.
The to-do list grows, its weight a burden,
Yet I find more excuses, of that I'm certain.

Oh, the joy of that fleeting release,
As I indulge in moments of inner peace.
But as the hours dwindle, guilt sets in,
Knowing I've let procrastination win.

Procrastination, my constant companion,
You lure me into your endless canyon.
Yet deep within, a voice cries out,
Urge me forward, quell my doubt.

For in the clutches of your embrace,
I lose sight of dreams I wish to chase.
No more shall I yield to your seductive call,
I'll break free from this self-made thrall.

Though the battle may be long and tough,
I'll rise above, I've had enough.
With each step forward, I'll find my stride,
And bid farewell to procrastination's tide.

For life's too short to waste away,
In the realm of "maybe" and "someday."
I'll seize the moment, with purpose and might,
And banish procrastination from my sight.

Autumn

As the crisp leaves fall,
Cold air slowly creeping in,
Autumn has landed.

Nana's Chutney

In Nana's kitchen, memories unfold,
Spicy tomato chutney, a taste so bold,
Childhood days, wrapped in its fiery embrace,
A cherished flavour that time cannot erase.

The crimson tomatoes, plump and ripe,
Sun-kissed sweetness, a delicious hype,
Nana's hands, skilled in the art of spice,
Creating a chutney, a flavour so nice.

The aroma, like a symphony of zest,
Tickling nostrils, an invitation to quest,
A dance of flavours, on taste buds it plays,
Igniting a fire, in nostalgic ways.

Oh, childhood memories, forever enshrined,
In Nana's spicy chutney, a taste divine,
A small jar of love, a treasure untold,
Nana's legacy, in each bite, I behold.

Finding Trust

Though full of doubt, a heart does yearn,
To trust once more, to let love return.
Oh, wounded soul, with scars yet unseen,
Longing for solace, where trust may convene.

Like fragile petals, scattered by wind,
Torn by past deceptions, love rescind.
But hope whispers softly, a gentle plea,
To open the gates, and set the heart free.

A sonnet forged in beauty and despair,
To heal the wounds, to mend what was unfair.
To gather strength, and let forgiveness flow,
With every beat, a new beginning will grow.

For in the depths of darkness, a light shines,
Renewing faith, trusting hearts intertwine.
Oh, wanting to trust again, let it start,
With open arms, embrace a brand new heart.

The magic of music

Music is magic, a spell cast upon our souls,
Unleashing emotions, making us whole.
It dances in the air, vibrating with grace,
Guiding us to places no words can trace.

In melodies, we find solace and peace,
A language transcending, granting release.
Through rhythm and harmony, hearts align,
Creating a symphony, divine and sublime.

It whispers secrets, hidden within each note,
Stirring memories, a timeless anecdote.
With every chord struck, it tells a tale,
A story of triumph, of love, and of hail.

Music is magic, a bridge to explore,
A portal to dreams, where nothing is more.
It heals our wounds, brings light to the dark,
Elevating spirits, igniting a spark.

In its embrace, we find solace and might,
A refuge of beauty, guiding us through the night.
So let the music play, let it take us away,
For within its enchantment, we'll forever stay.

It wasn't just you I lost

Long before I lost you, I lost myself.
Continued to put my own needs on a shelf.
Locked deep in my mind, pushed as far as
they'd go;
I tried to silence those demons and move on with
the show.
Dreaming of bigger and better or just what's
right,
A fantasy by day but alone by night.
All those years just didn't seem real,
You really never understood how I feel.
I feel things deep and bold and true,
I convinced myself it was worth it for you.
You took my loyalty and my commitment, my
desires and shames,
Only to throw them into the flames.
When all is said and done, I know this to be true;
You never loved me in the way I loved you.
You loved me for how I love, what I gave or did,
But in the end your true self, that you had hid.

All the lies and the cheating, those things I
ignored.
You only loved me until you got bored.
I was broken and hurt, so lost and alone.
You stripped me bare, down to the bone.
Yet still the the love, it poured out of my soul;
Holding onto the belief that it'd make me feel
whole.
It may have taken eight long years for me to see.
That pouring all that love into you, was slowly
killing me.

Unconditional

In the realm of love, where hearts entwine,
There exists a bond, so pure, so divine.
Where wagging tails and soft, gentle eyes,
Speak a language, untamed and wise.

Dogs, the guardians of loyalty and truth,
With every wag, they offer us proof,
Of a love so pure, unconditionally bestowed,
A love that fills our hearts, it overflows.

With paws that dance, on paths untrod,
They teach us to live, to trust, to applaud.
For in their presence, we find solace and peace,
A gentle reminder that love will never cease.

Through darkest nights and stormy days,
They stand beside us, in countless ways.
Their unwavering love, an eternal flame,
Igniting hope and wiping away all shame.

Their eyes, mirrors of a love so deep,
A love that asks for nothing, but to keep,
Our hearts open, our souls ablaze,
With gratitude for the love they raise.

So let us cherish these creatures divine,
Their love, a treasure, forever mine.
For in their presence, we learn to forgive,
And embrace the beauty of life as we live.

In the realm of love, where hearts entwine,
Dogs teach us the meaning of love so fine.
Unconditional, faithful, a love like no other,
A gift from above, forever and ever.

Starting over

In shadows cast by the mistakes I've made,
A glimmer of hope beckons me to rise,
To shed the past, where darkness gently fades,
And let my spirit soar, unburdened skies.

With tender grace, the dawn begins anew,
A chance to mend the fragments of my soul,
To paint my world with colours bright and true,
And step beyond the boundaries of old.

This journey calls for courage, strong and pure,
To trust the path that lies ahead, unknown,
Embrace the lessons learned, endure, endure,
And carve a destiny that's mine alone.

For life's sweet symphony is not in vain,
In starting over, we find strength to reign.

A sky full of stars

Stars, beautiful and bright,
Sprinkled across the canvas of night.
Infinite in number, yet distant and far,
They twinkle and shimmer, like celestial
memoirs.

Each a tiny flicker, a beacon of light,
Guiding lost souls through the darkest of nights.
They dance and they soar, in a cosmic ballet,
A mesmerising spectacle, on display.

Some burn fiercely, with a radiant hue,
While others are dim, barely breaking through.
But together they form a tapestry divine,
A celestial masterpiece, so sublime.

They whisper secrets, untold and profound,
Their stories woven into the night's gown.
They witness the triumphs, the joys, and the
pain,
Silent witnesses to the human refrain.

Stars, beautiful and distant,
Their wisdom spanning time, persistent.
They remind us of our place in the grand design,
A part of something greater, a cosmic sign.

So, let us gaze up at the night sky,
And marvel at the stars, as they pass us by.
For in their brilliance, we find solace and peace,
A reminder that beauty will never cease.

Fickle Fate

They say it is inevitable,
Just stuck there in time.
Inevitability keeping it still,
steady and in line.
Just waiting for the right soul
to come passing along.
Uncontrollable and unsure,
Yet set in stone.
Whether big or small,
It's one thing for sure.
Predetermined and unmoving;
It's totally unknown.
Not fazed by belief,
Nor hope or trust.

Coming for you, regardless of what you lust.
Despite your desires,
Your hunger and greed.
Trust that it will bring exactly what you need.
Yes it's fickle, often seen as a woe;
But fate will guide you to where you should go.
Like an old friend watching you blossom from a
seed;
Yes, it's fickle…
But a friend indeed.

Under the light of the full moon.

When the moon shines so bright,
It's just like sunlight.
But you can still see the stars,
Up there, in that dark night sky.
Though you stand on your own,
You know in an instant,
you're never alone.
As a magical feeling washes over your soul,
Like something is telling you where you should
go.

Connected and grounded throughout the night,
That star-struck feeling you cannot fight.
Looking up at the sky, you know you are home,
Just a collection of energy from the great
unknown.
As much as you are, though small you may be,
Right here, right now, you are free.
Under the great expanse of that moonlit sky,
You feel safe and content, just knowing why.
Why you are here and why you are you,
It's then you know,
It's not just out there;
The universe itself; lies within you too.